THE CRITTER CUBE BOOK

I Drew the Pictures - You Write the Story

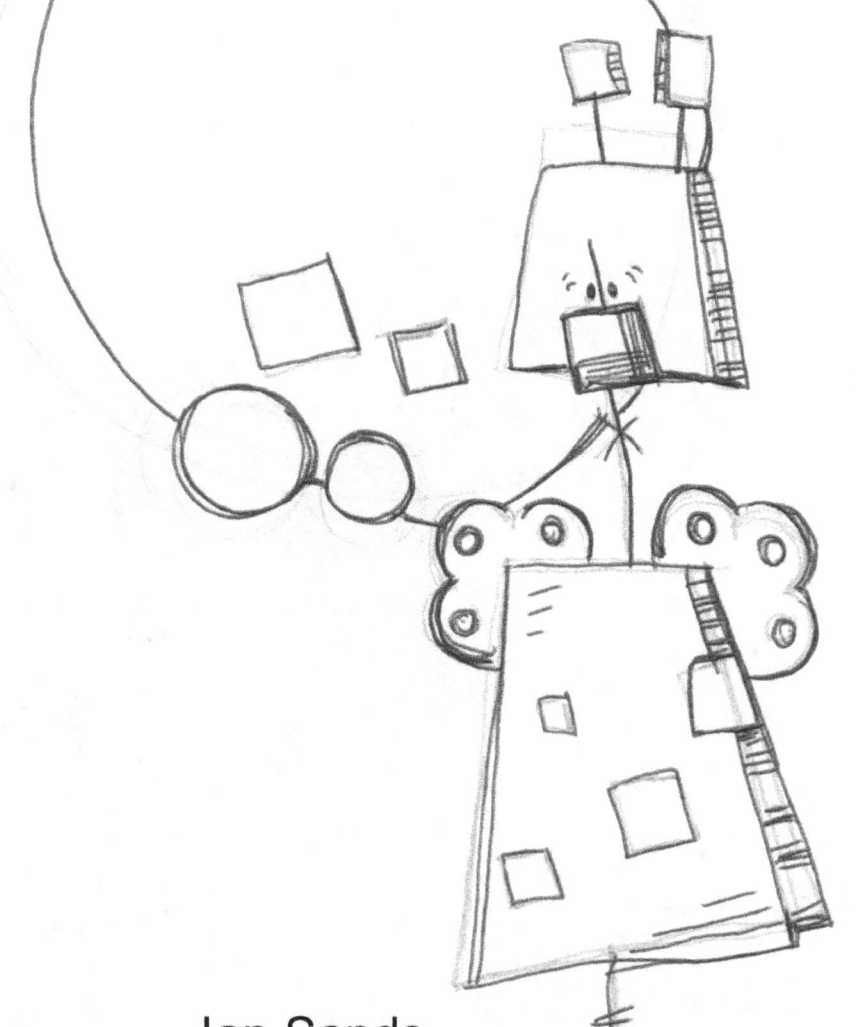

Ian Sands

project of The Graham Johnson Cultural Arts Endowment

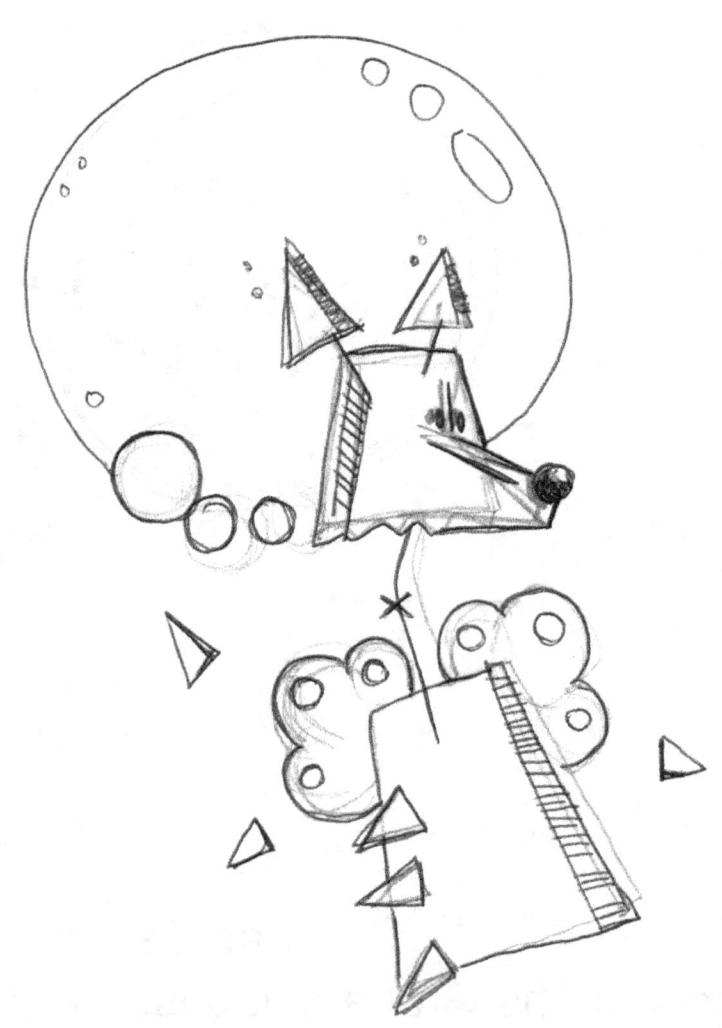

HOW IT WORKS...

I drew the pictures, you write the story. To help you out,
This book contains three sections.

In section one you'll be introduced to five Critter Cube
characters. It'll be up to you to define their personalities.

In section two you'll write a story. Each page of this section
contains a brief writing prompt to offer some story direction.
You can deviate from the prompt as little or as much as you
want... After all, it's your story.

Section three is just like the Critter Cubes but in book form.
Grab a scissor and cut along the dotted lines. Then you can
mix and match and create your own critters and sentences.

You might have noticed this book is in black and white.
That's sort of boring. It would be a lot more colorful if you
colored it. I'm sure crayons or markers would work fine.

Now get to it!

Ian Sands
M@KE @RT!
http://www.zonkeystreet.com

SECTION ONE...

In this section you'll be introduced to five Critter Cube characters. It's up to you to define their personalities.

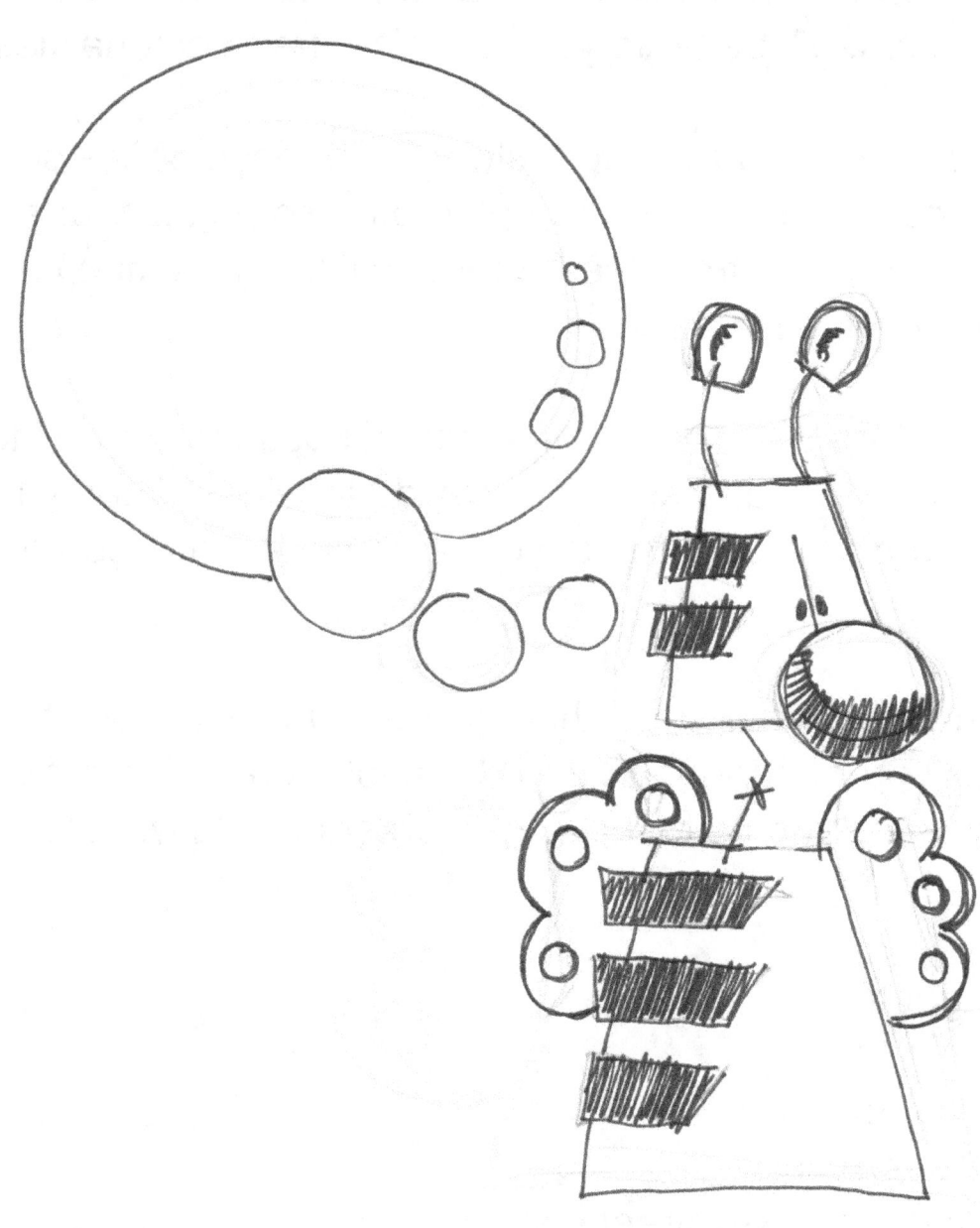

Name:_____

Age:_____

Hobbies: _____

Dislikes: _____

Strenghts:_____

Weaknesses:_____

Favortie Food:_____

Best Friend:_____

Name:_____

Age:_____

Hobbies: _____

Dislikes: _____

Strenghts:_____

Weaknesses:_____

Favortie Food:_____

Best Friend:_____

Name:_____

Age:_____

Hobbies: _____

Dislikes: _____

Strenghts:_____

Weaknesses:_____

Favortie Food:_____

Best Friend:_____

Name:_____

Age:_____

Hobbies: _____

Dislikes: _____

Strenghts:_____

Weaknesses:_____

Favortie Food:_____

Best Friend:_____

Name:_____

Age:_____

Hobbies: _____

Dislikes: _____

Strenghts:_____

Weaknesses:_____

Favortie Food:_____

Best Friend:_____

SECTION TWO...

In this section you'll write a story. Each page of this section contains a brief writing prompt to offer some story direction. You can deviate from the prompt as little or as much as you want... After all, it's your story.

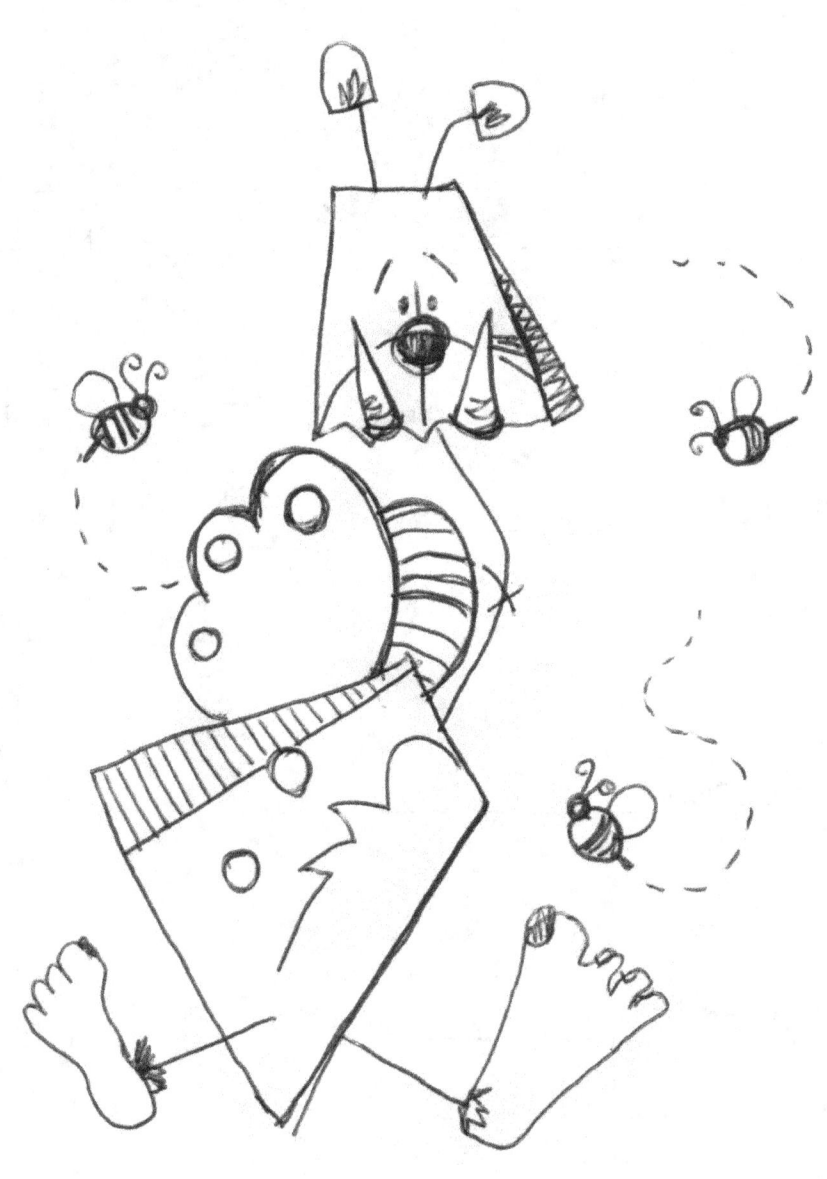

Once upon a time
there was a critter

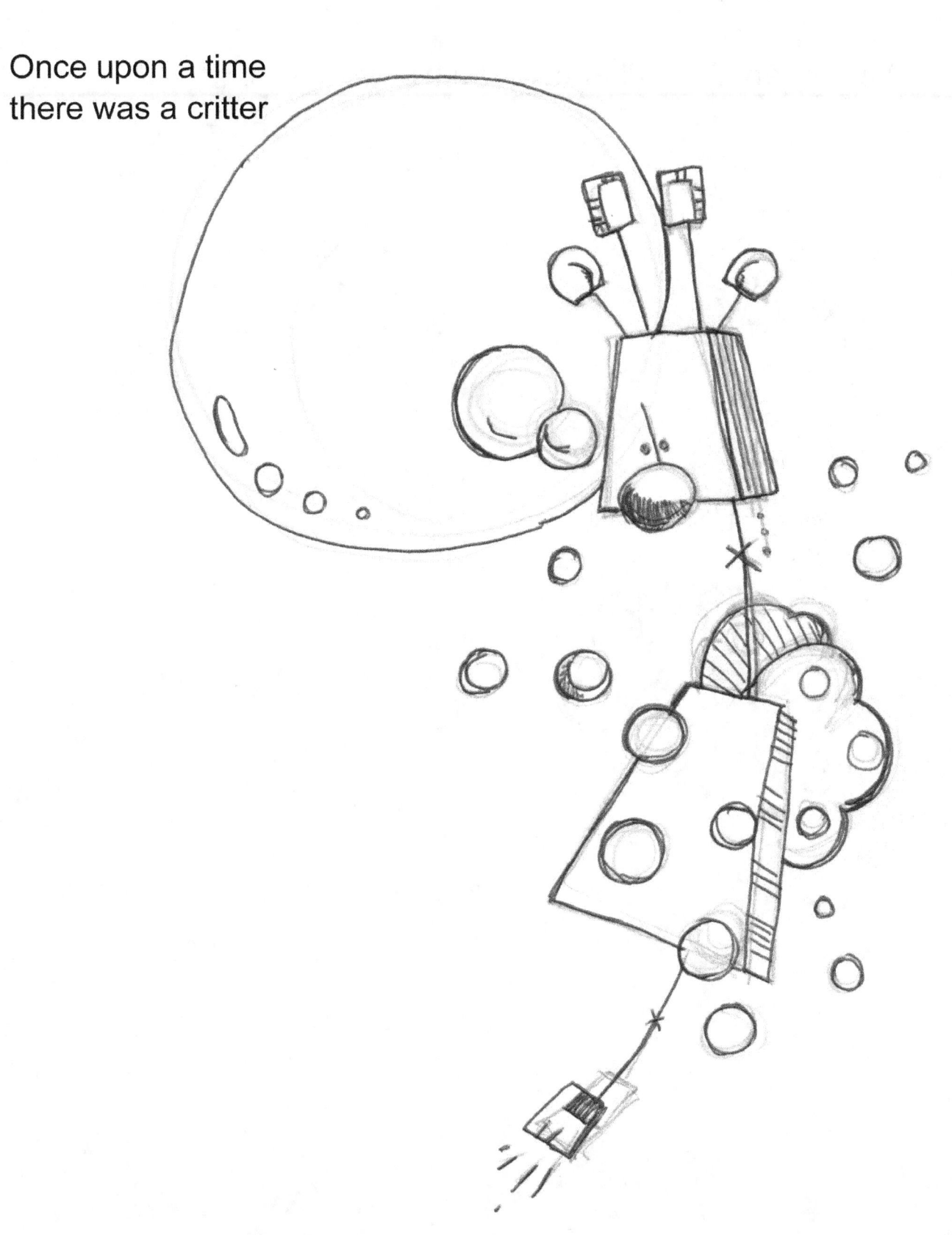

One day another critter came with some news.

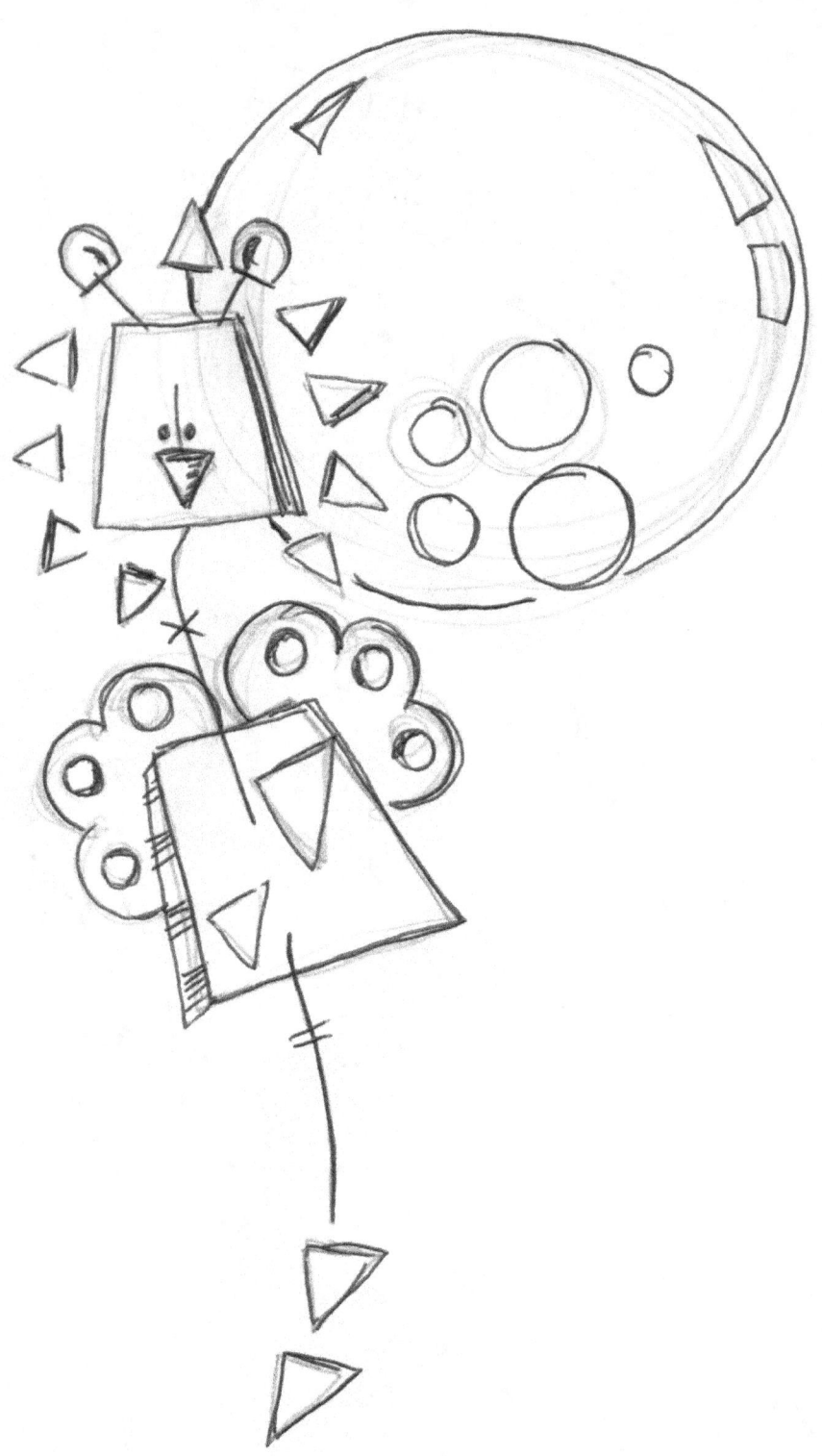

When Critter heard the
news he immediately
went to

When Critter arrived he learned that.

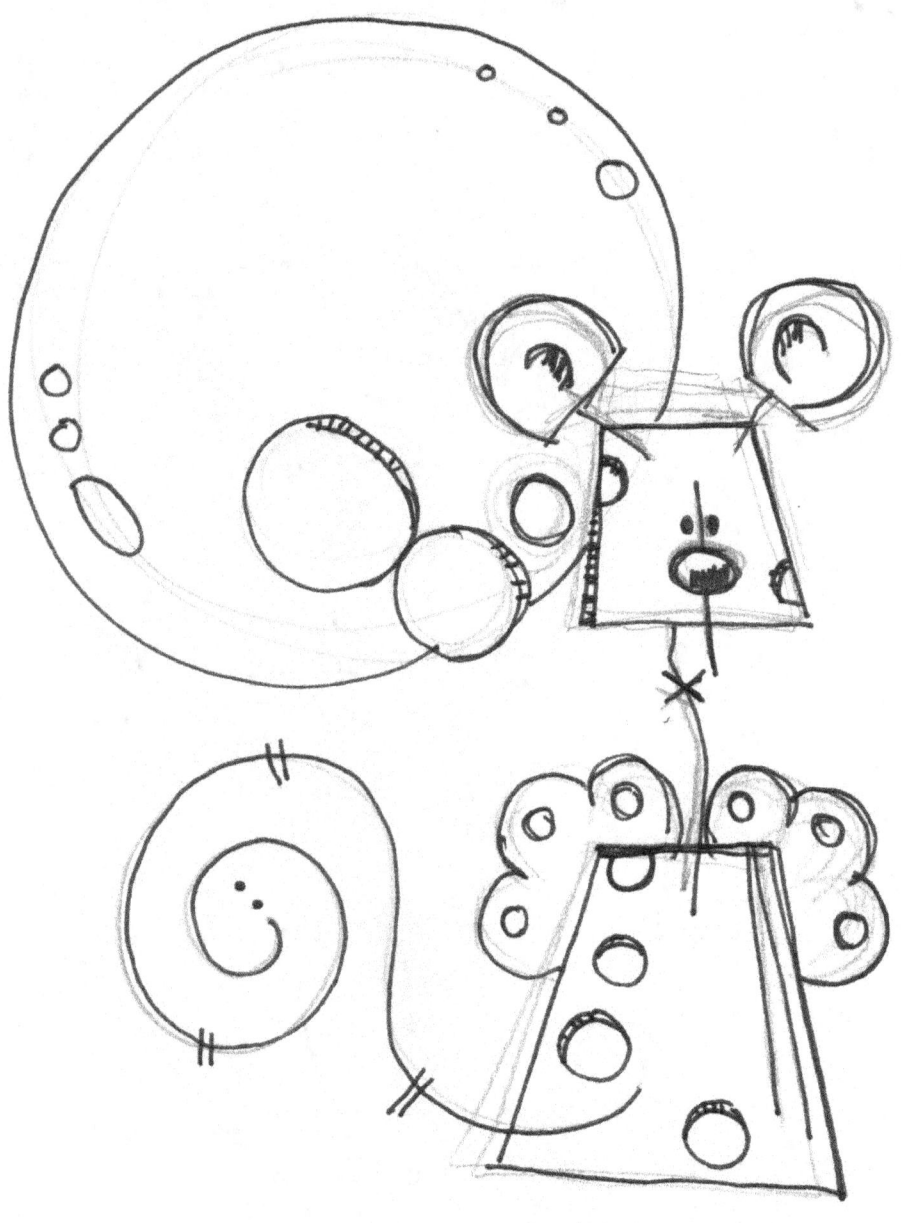

Critter made a plan.

Critter's plan would have worked but nobody expected

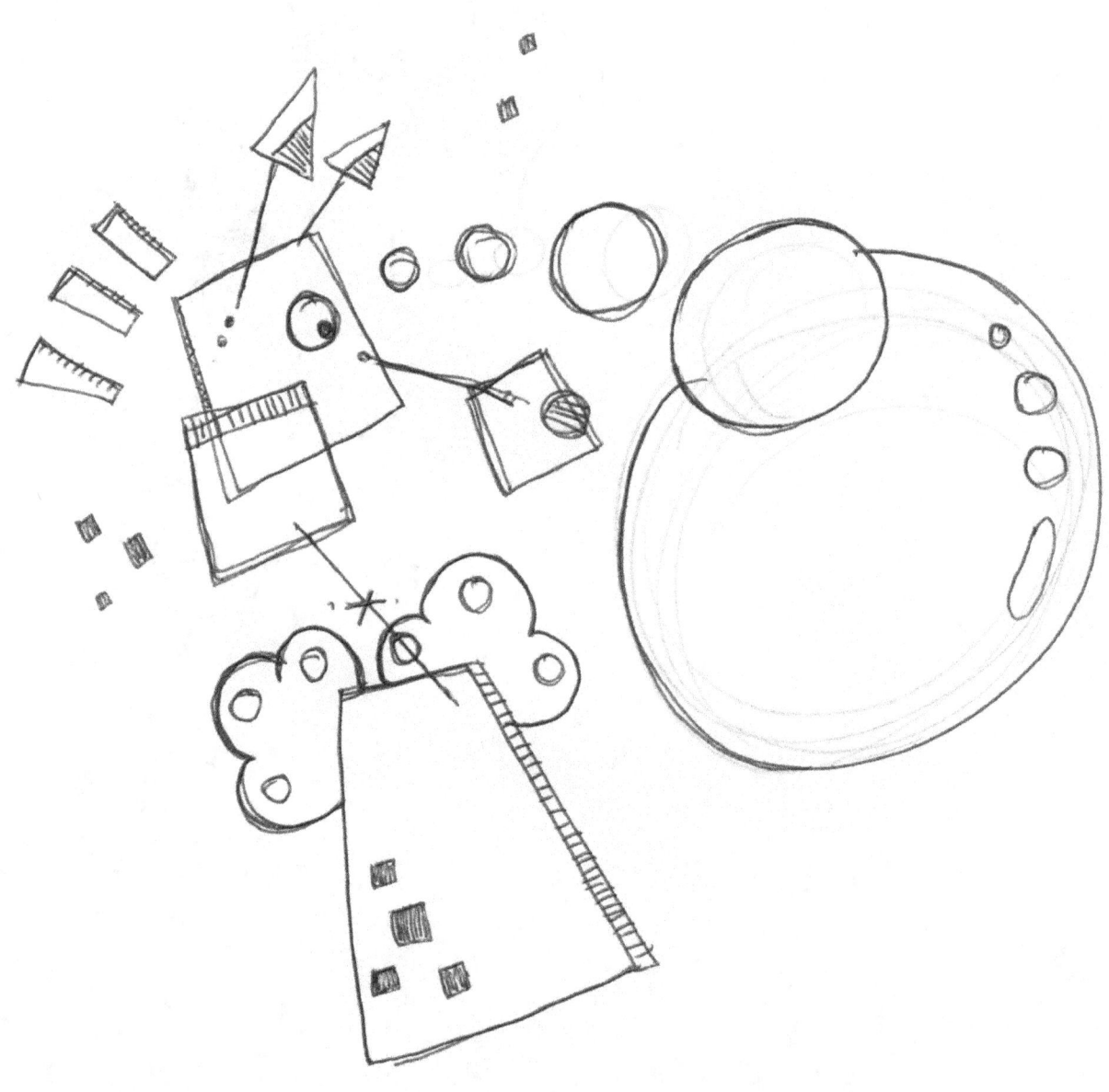

Critter knew what he must do.

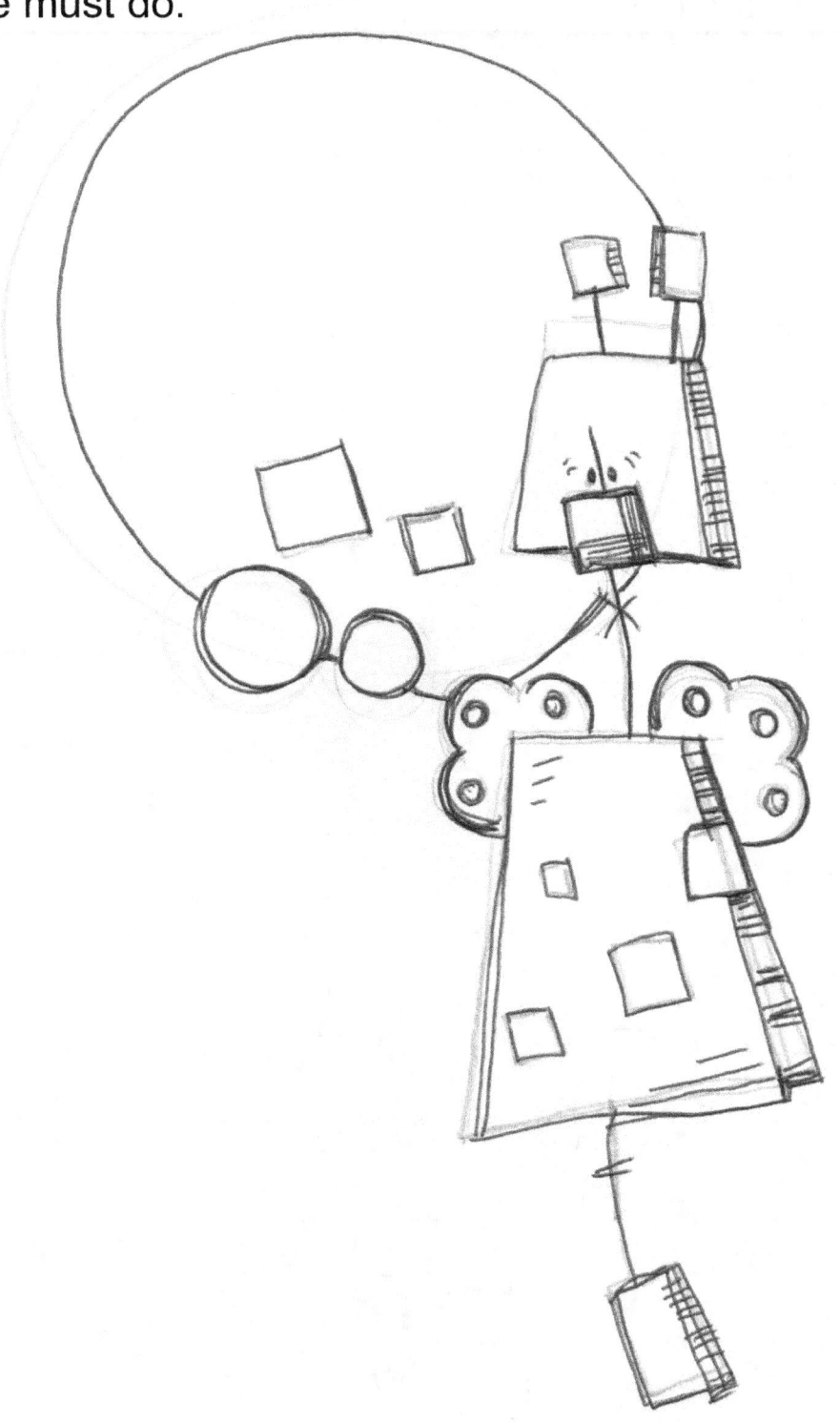

In the end

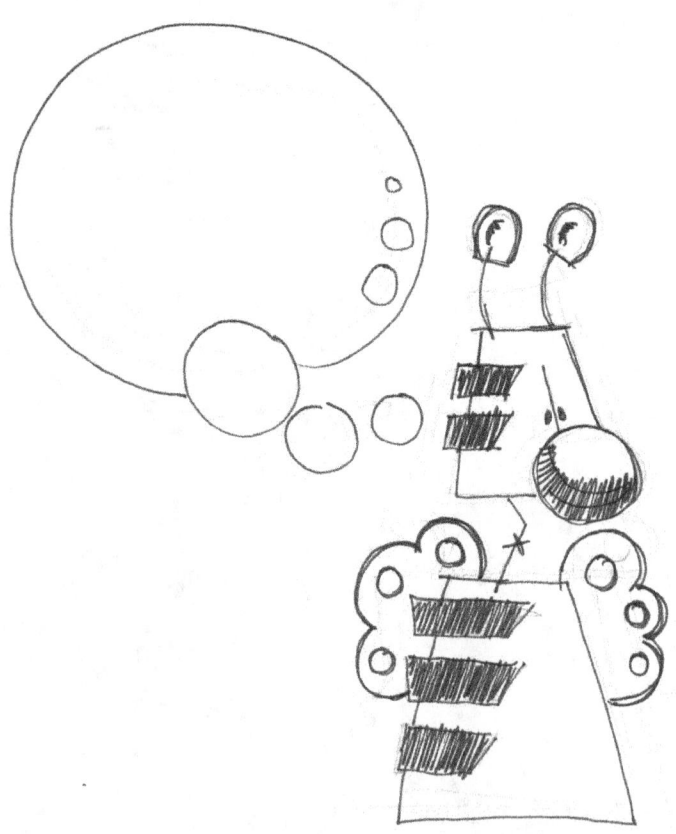

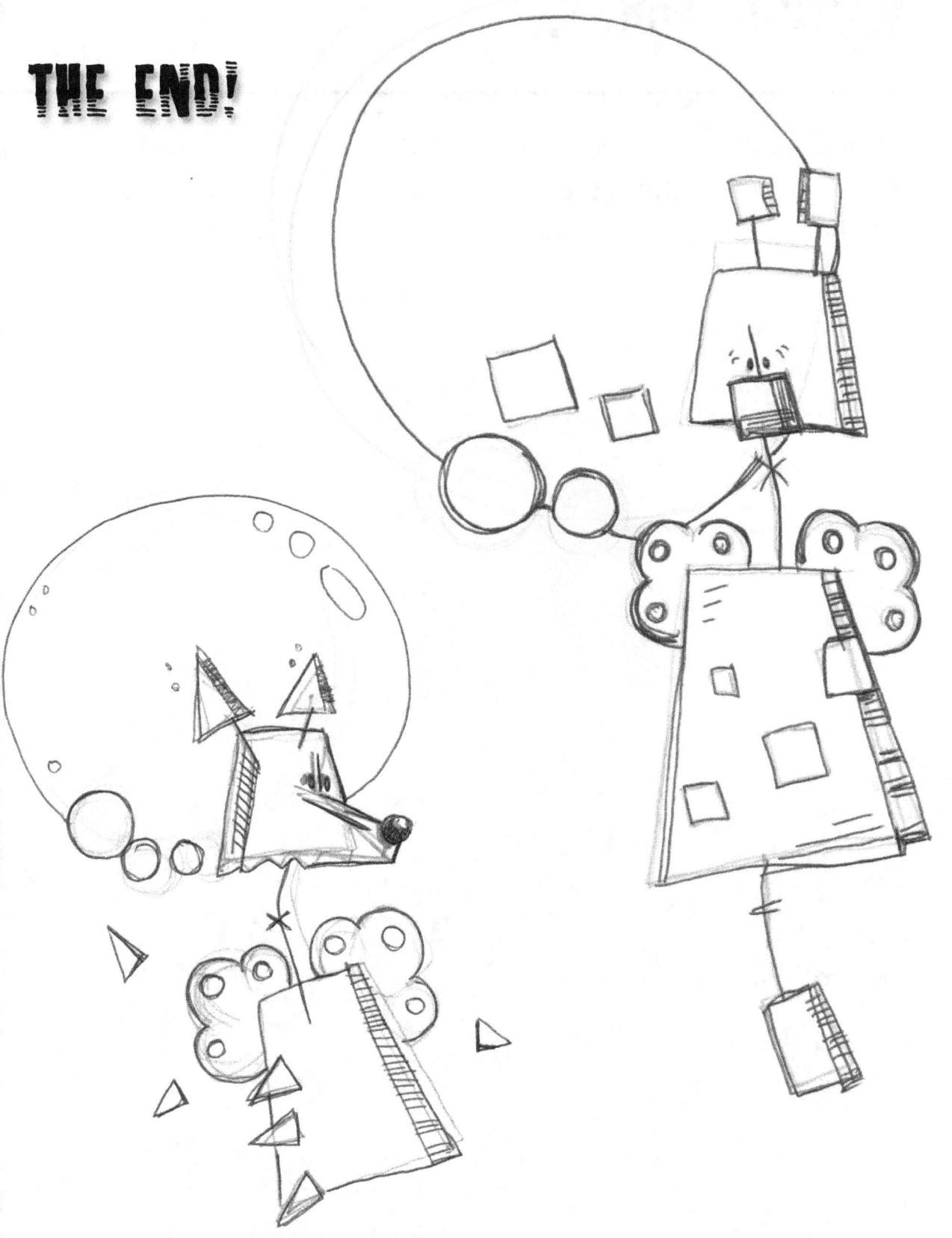

SECTION THREE...

Section three is just like the Critter Cubes but in book form. Grab a scissor and cut along the dotted lines. Then you can mix and match the pictures to create your own critters and add your own words to create your own sentences!

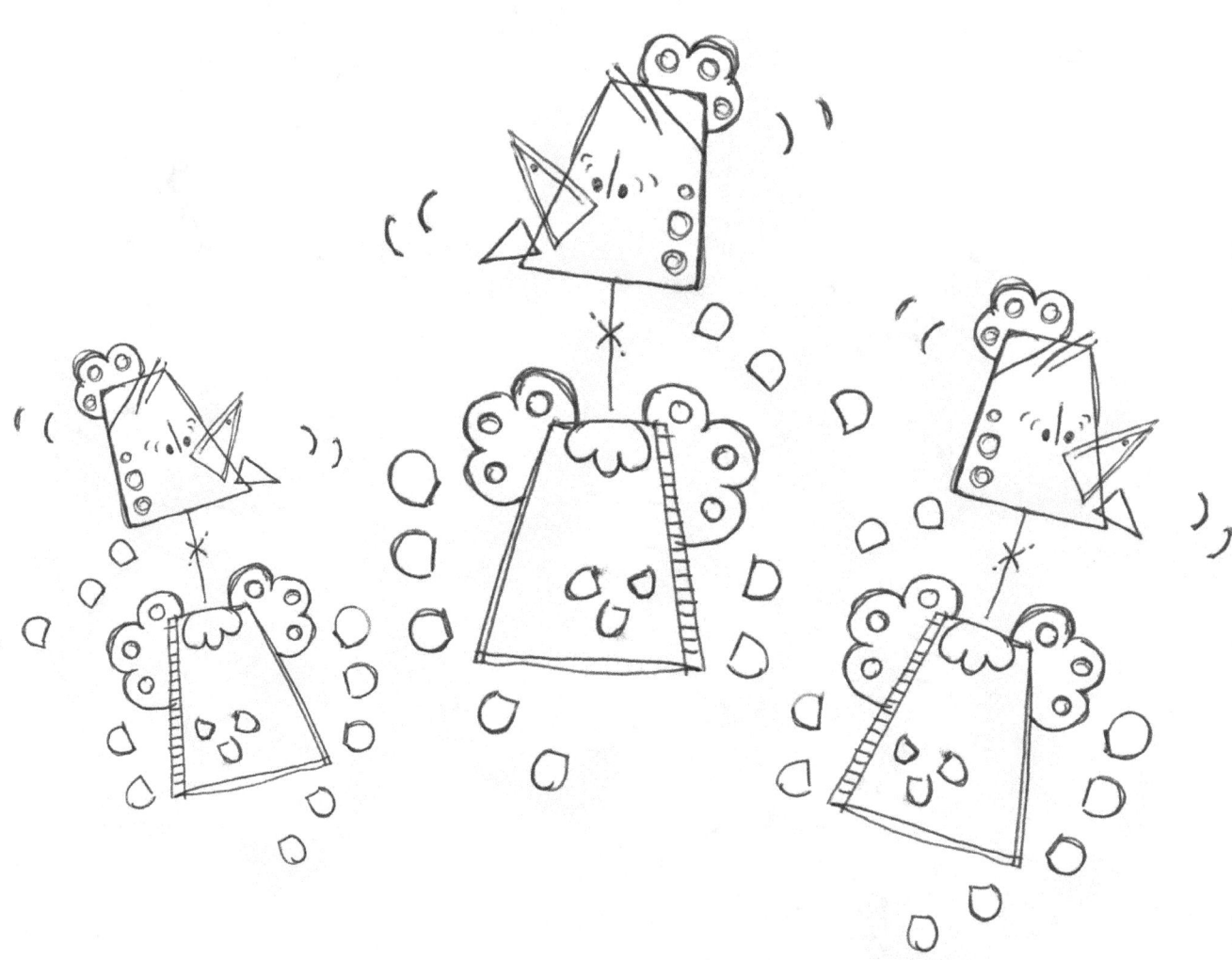

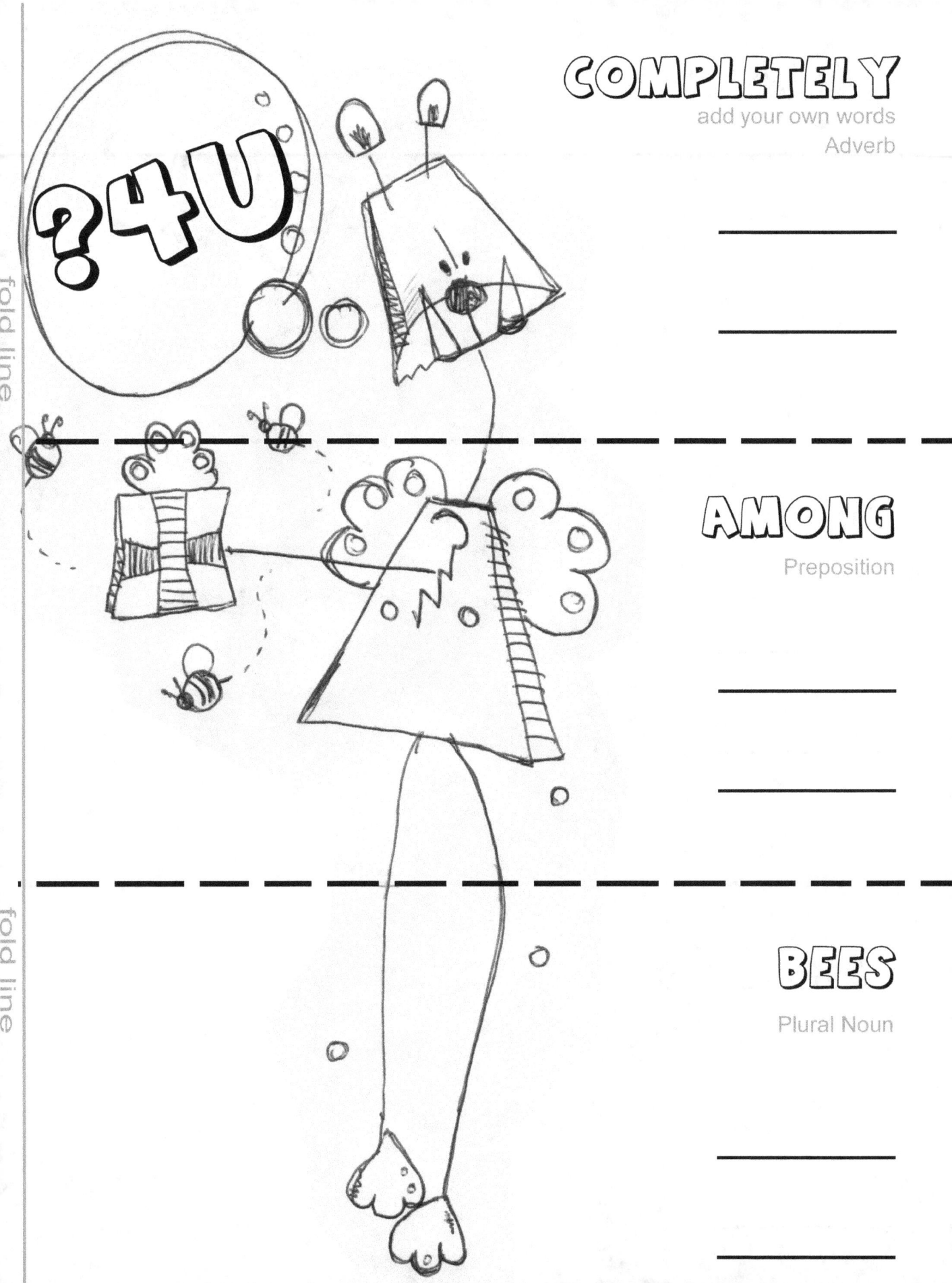

COMPLETELY
add your own words
Adverb

_____

_____

AMONG
Preposition

_____

_____

BEES
Plural Noun

_____

_____

fold line

fold line

BEARS

add your own words
Plural Noun

_____

_____

FLOAT

Verb

_____

_____

JEALOUS

Adjective

_____

_____

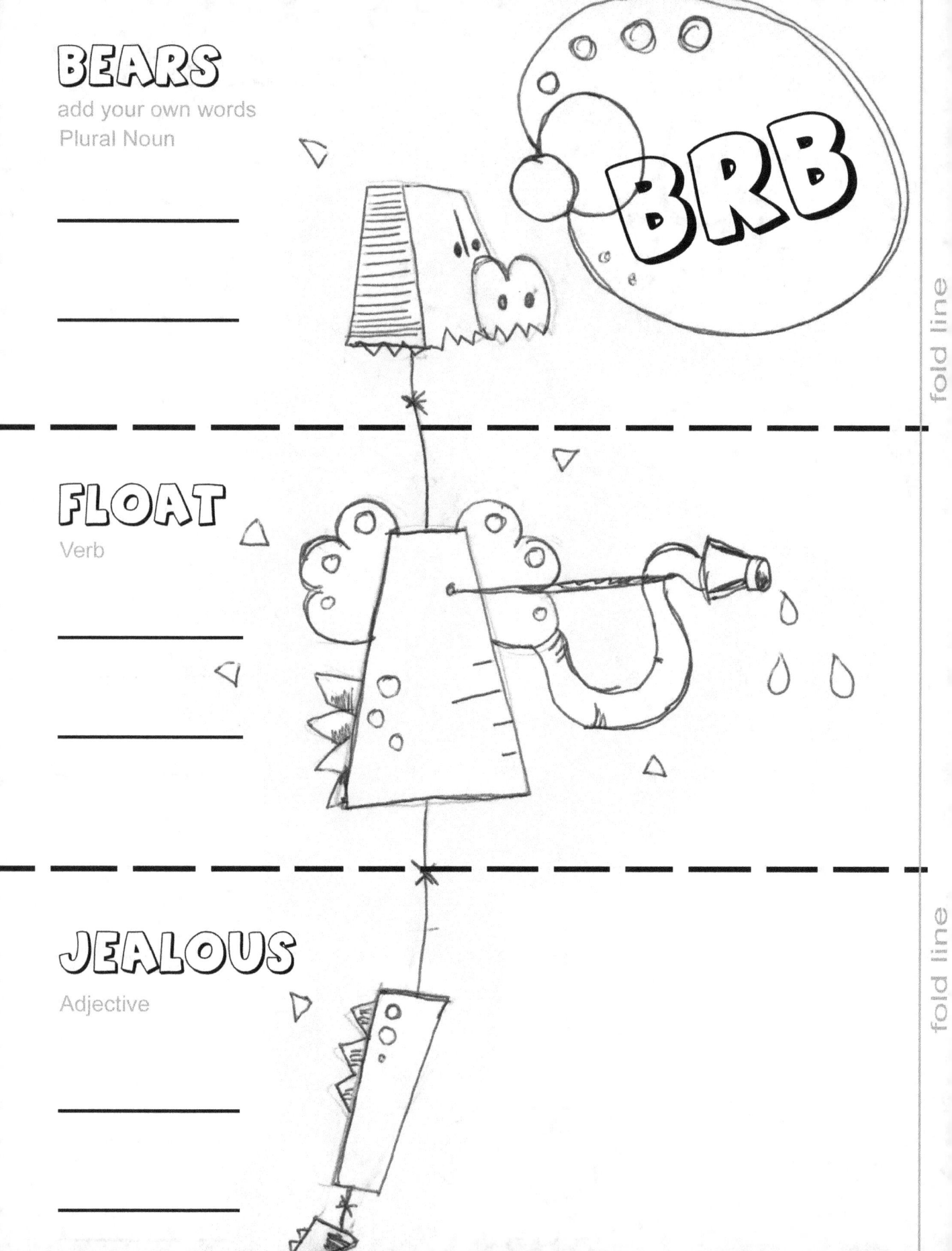

fold line

fold line

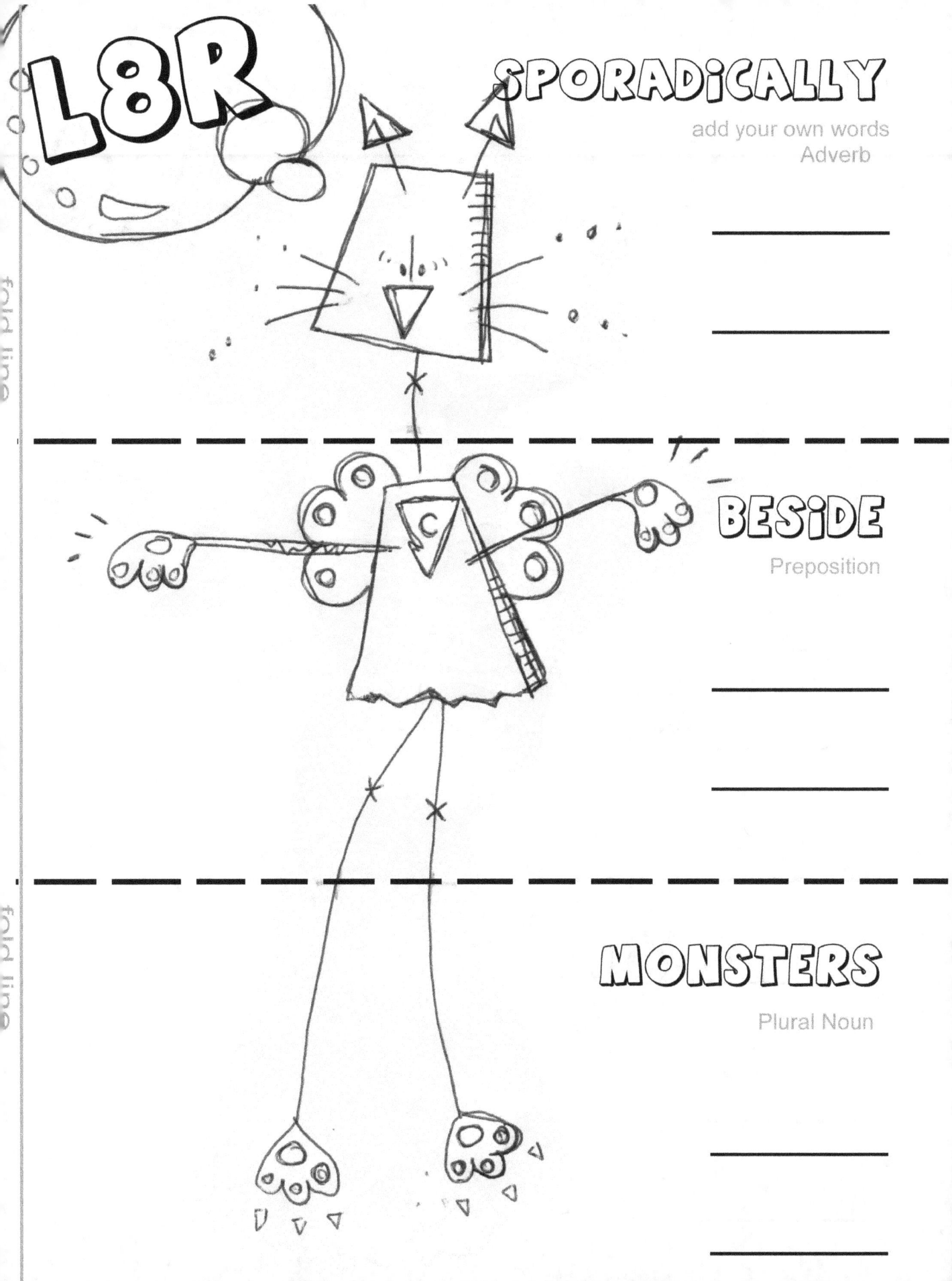

SPORADICALLY

add your own words
Adverb

_____

_____

BESIDE

Preposition

_____

_____

MONSTERS

Plural Noun

_____

_____

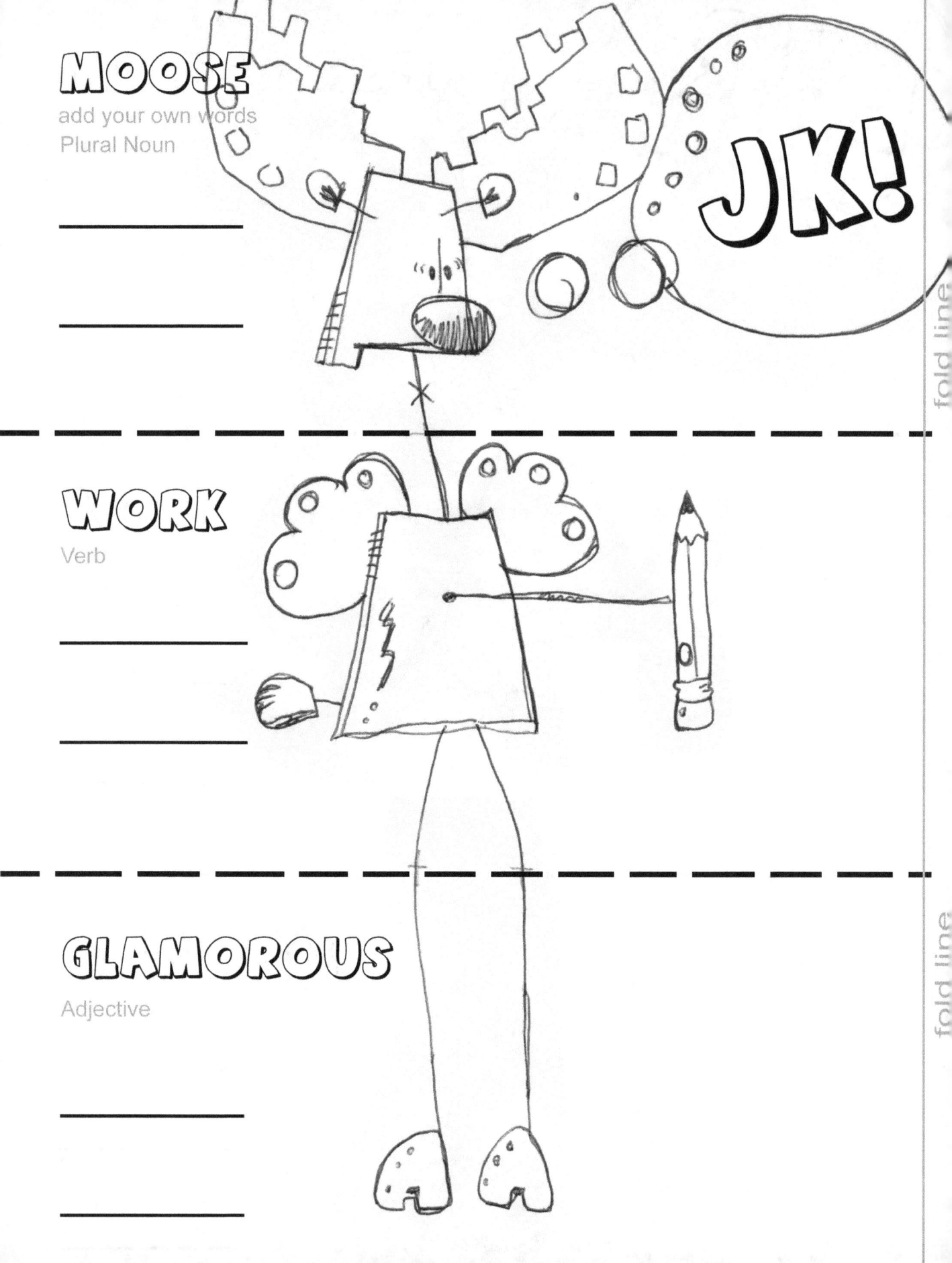

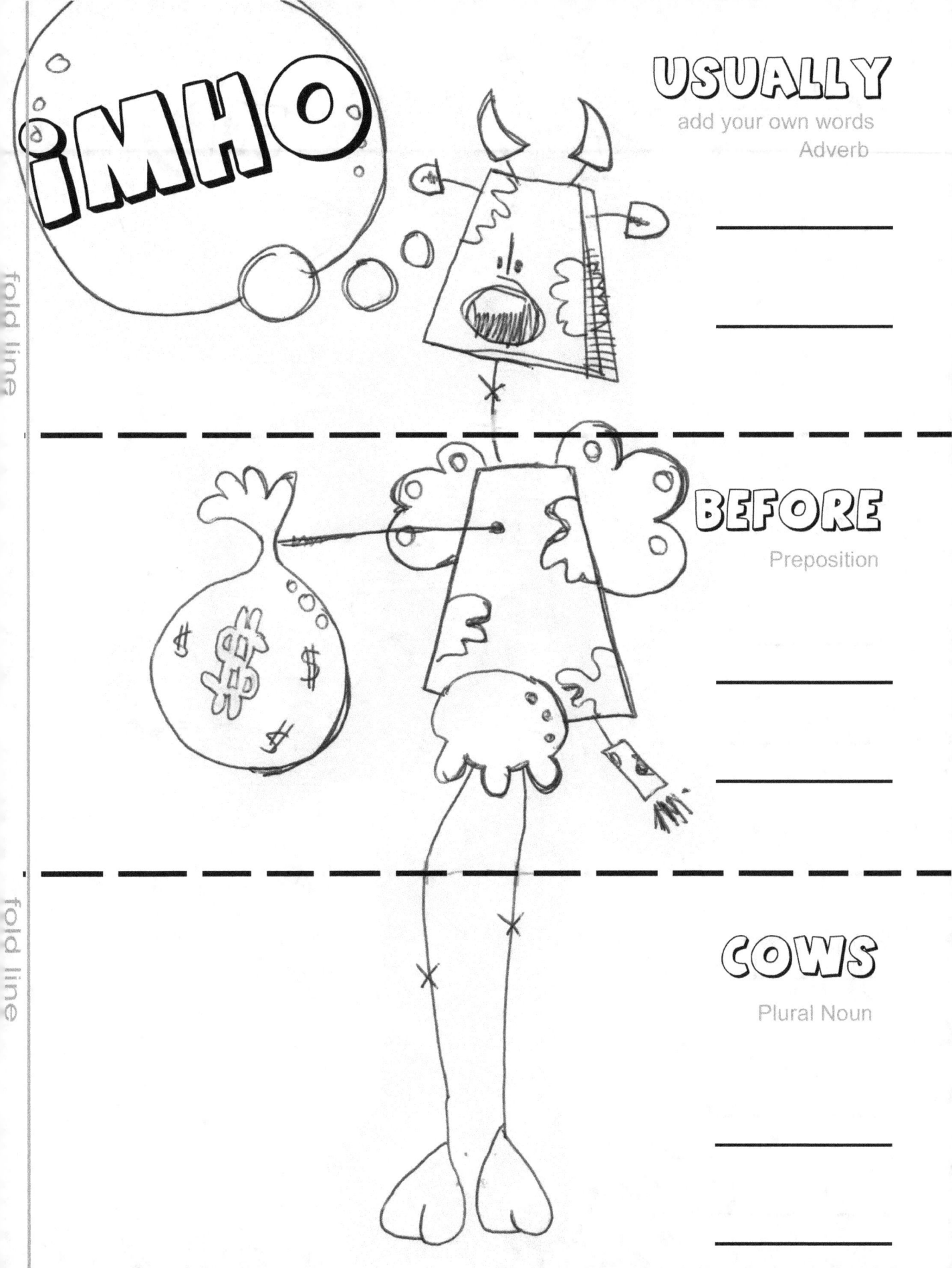

USUALLY

add your own words

Adverb

_____

_____

BEFORE

Preposition

_____

_____

COWS

Plural Noun

_____

_____

ZONKEYS

add your own words

Plural Noun

_____

_____

THiNK

Verb

_____

_____

SiLLY

Adjective

_____

_____

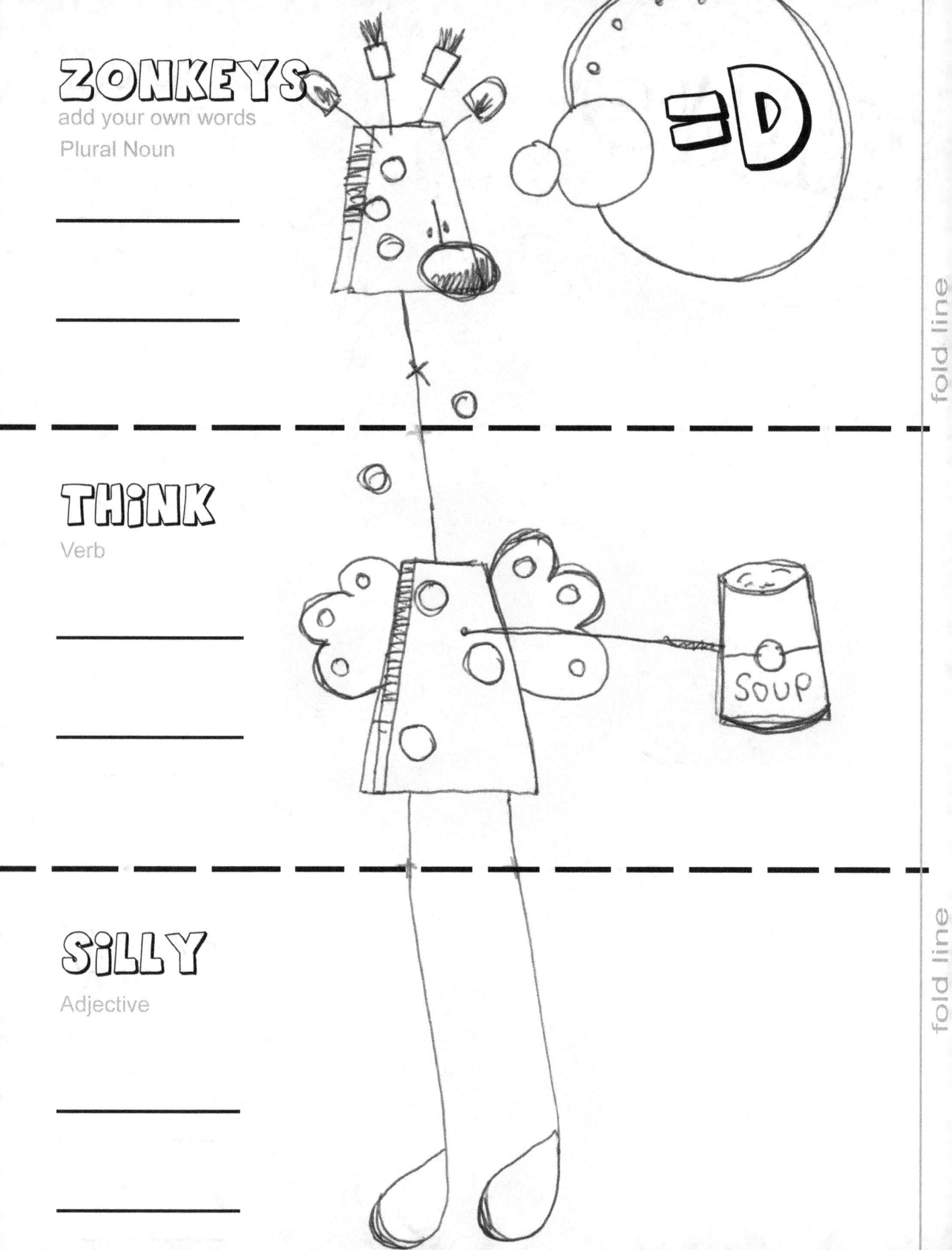

SOUP

=D

fold line

fold line

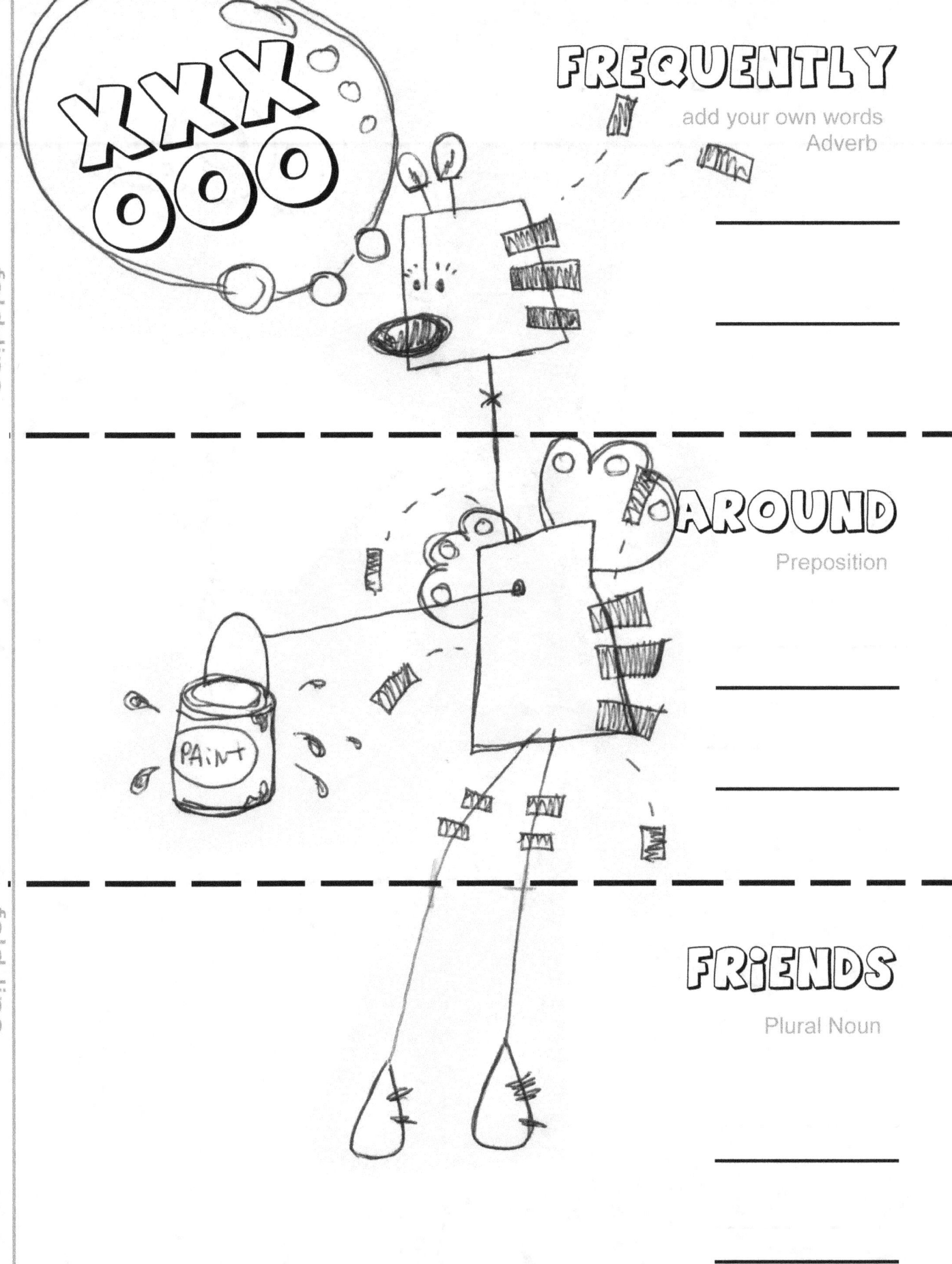

FREQUENTLY

add your own words
Adverb

_____

_____

AROUND

Preposition

_____

_____

FRIENDS

Plural Noun

_____

_____

fold line

fold line

ALLiGATORS

add your own words
Plural Noun

_____

_____

TALK

Verb

_____

_____

OBNOXiOUS

Adjective

_____

_____

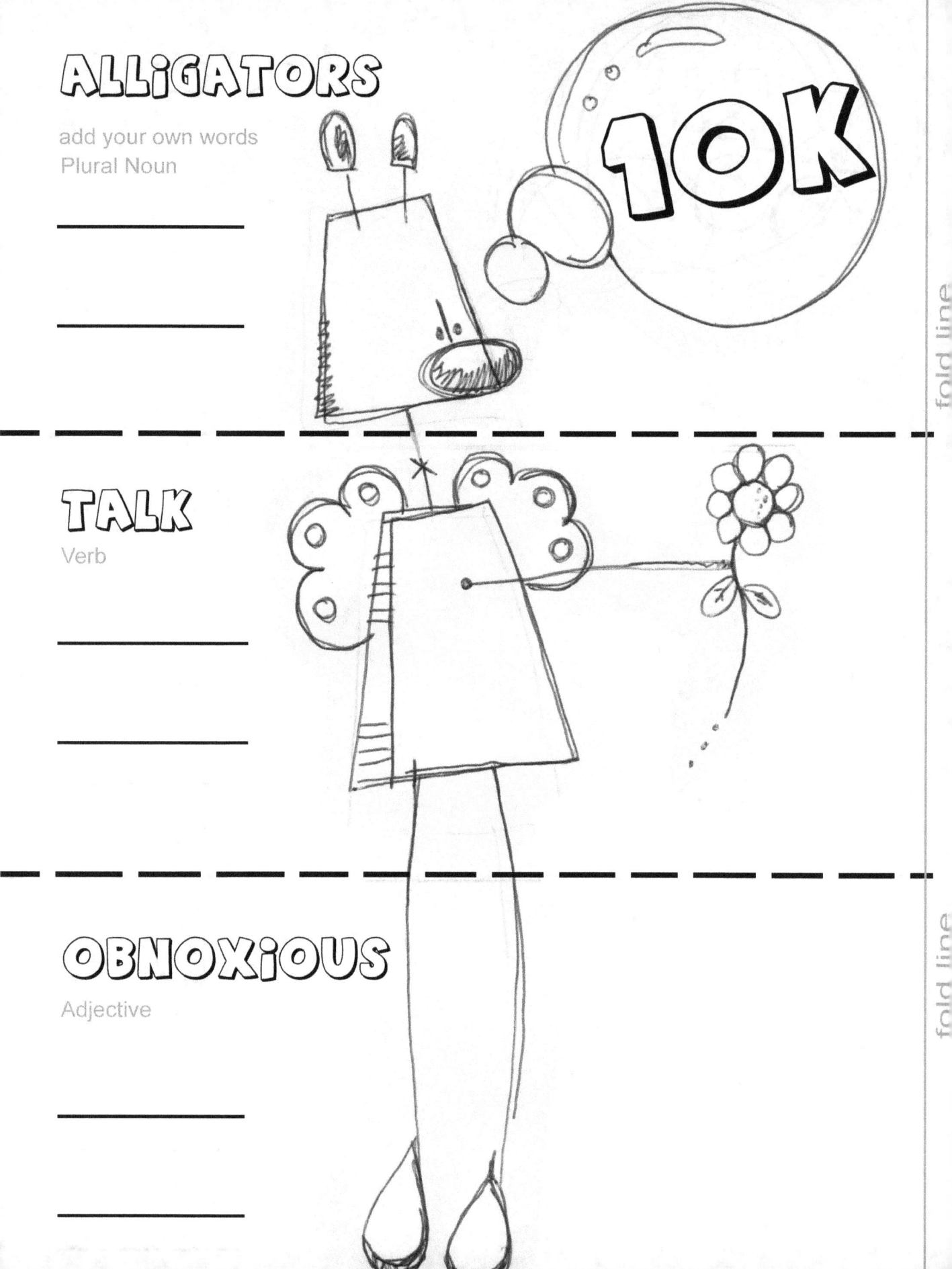

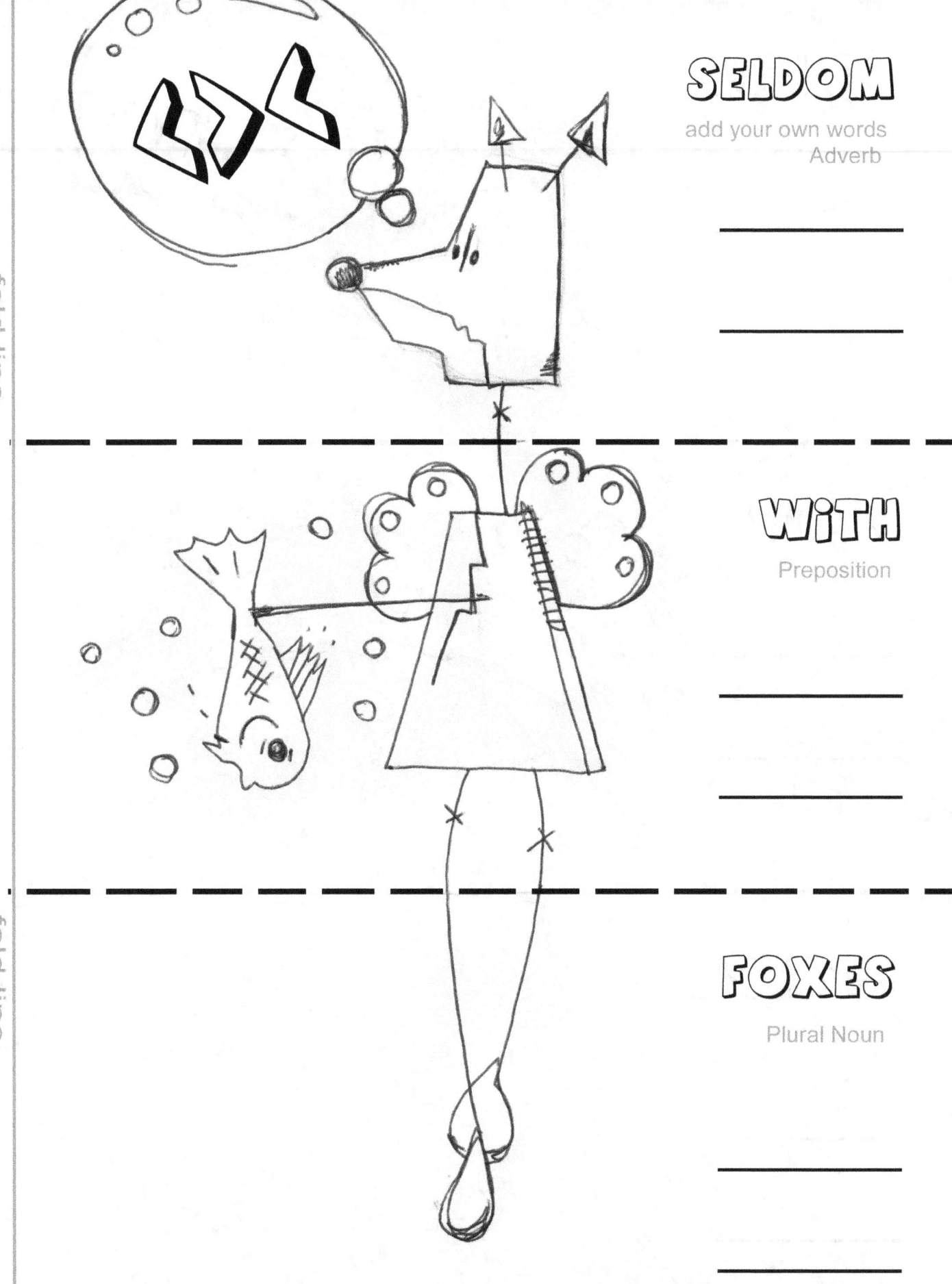

SELDOM

add your own words
Adverb

_____

_____

WiTH

Preposition

_____

_____

FOXES

Plural Noun

_____

_____

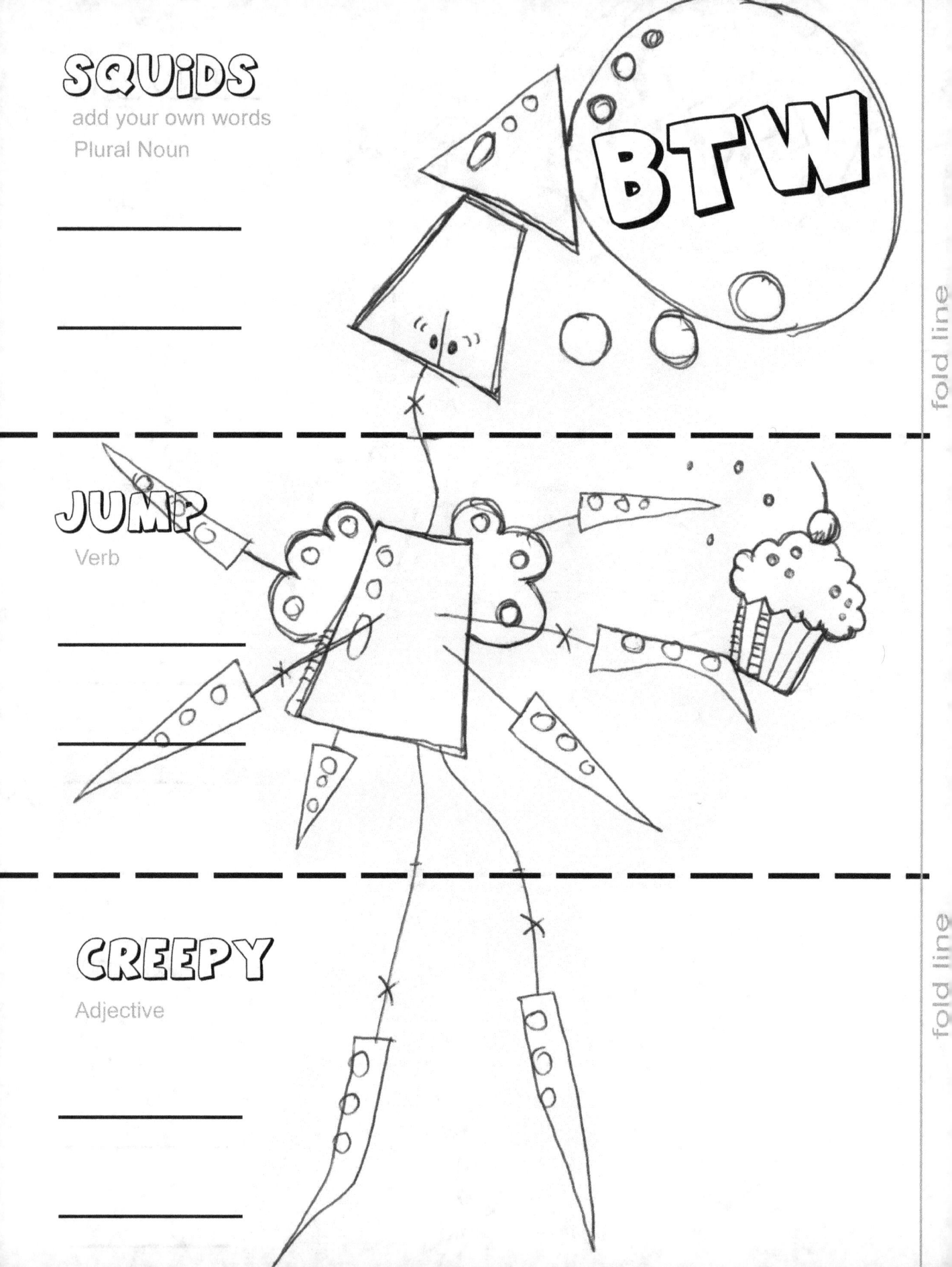

SQUIDS

add your own words

Plural Noun

_____

_____

JUMP

Verb

_____

_____

CREEPY

Adjective

_____

_____

BTW

fold line

fold line

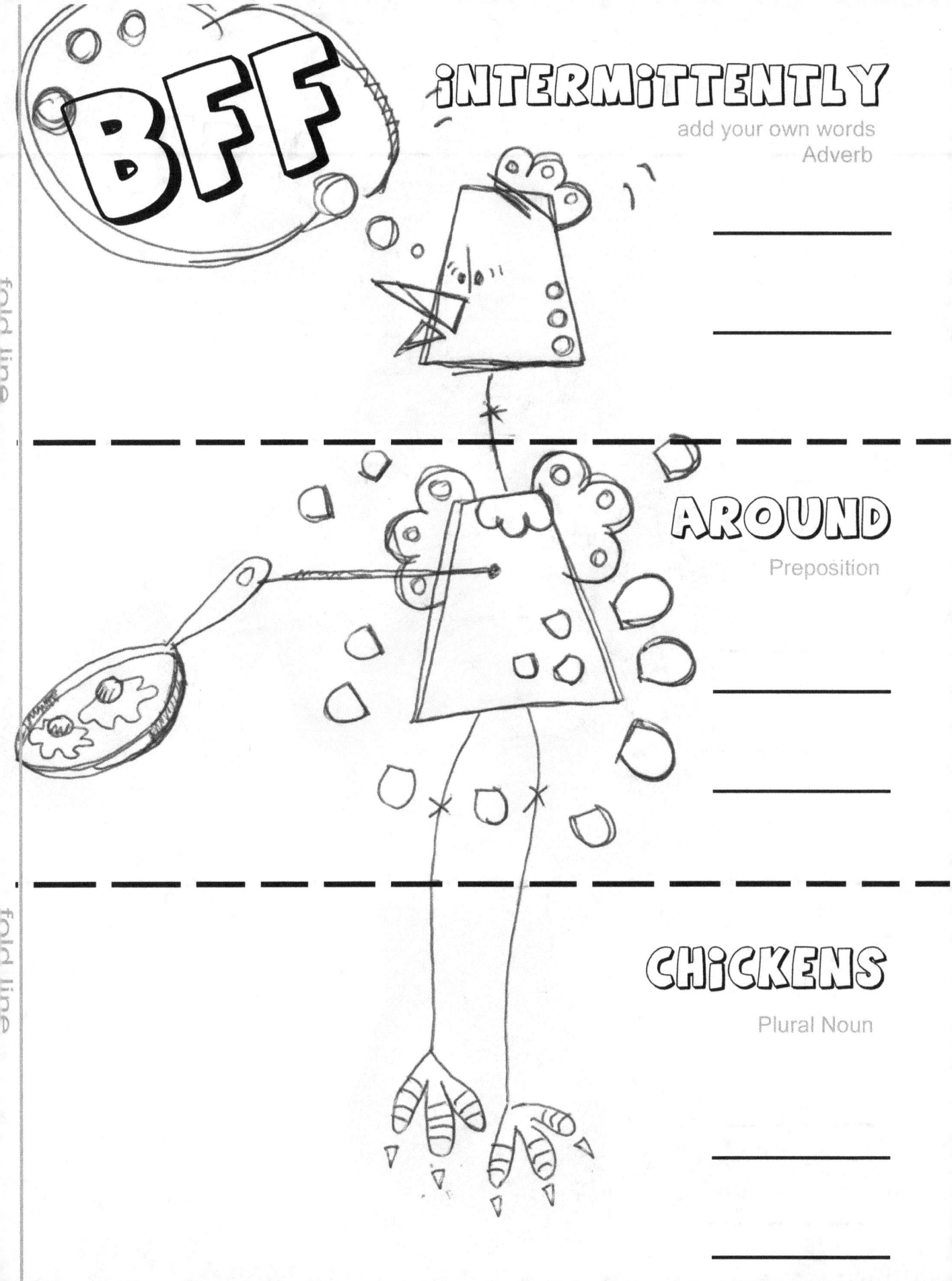

BFF

INTERMITTENTLY
add your own words
Adverb

_____

_____

AROUND
Preposition

_____

_____

CHICKENS
Plural Noun

_____

_____

fold line

fold line

TURTLES

add your own words
Plural Noun

_____

_____

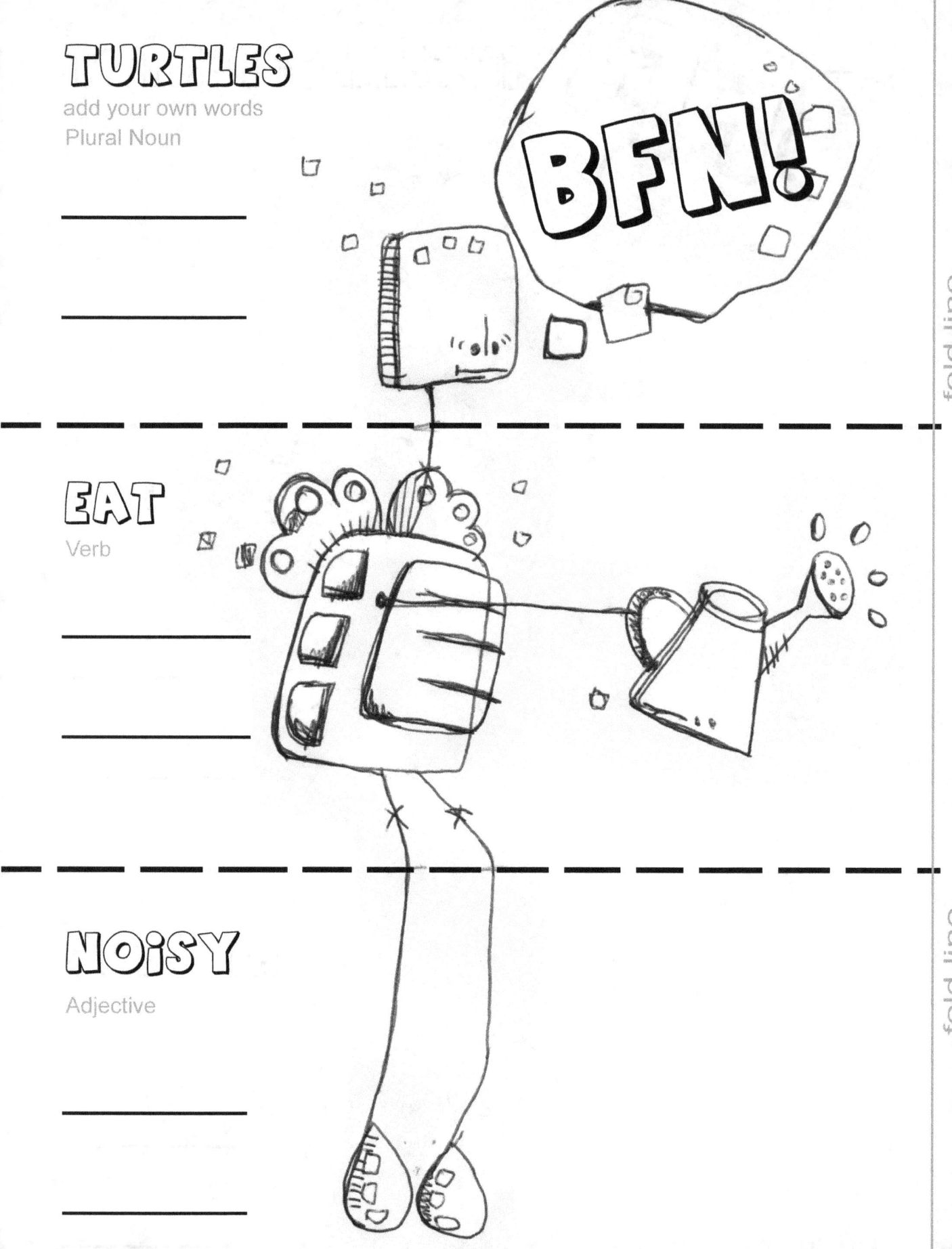

EAT

Verb

_____

_____

NOiSY

Adjective

_____

_____

fold line

fold line